This book is dedicated to all members of Supon Design Group whose considerable efforts and unwavering dedication do not go unnoticed.

—Supon Phornirunlit

Design Editions

ISBN 1-889491-05-5

Library of Congress Catalog Card Number 96-70988

Distributed to the trade in the United Stated, Canada,
and Mexico by:
Book Nippan
1123 Dominguez Street, Unit K
Carson, CA 90746
Fax (310) 604.1134

Published by:
Design Editions
1700 K Street, NW, Suite 400
Washington, DC 20006
Phone (202) 822.6540
Fax (202) 822.6541

Printed in Hong Kong

DESIGN WISE

WARNING: Use of this book may be hazardous to preconceptions, injurious to bad taste, and may increase your recognition of excellence in design.

Project & Creative Director:
Supon Phornirunlit

Jacket Designer:
Mimi Eanes

Book Designers:
Dujdao "Pum" Mek-aroonreung
Mimi Eanes

Project Director:
Deborah Savitt

Editors:
Wayne Kurie
Greg Varner

Agent for Rights & Marketing:
Henry Kornman, HK Marketing Services

Photographer:
Oi Veerasarn

As thousands of designers can tell you, they are in the business of solving their clients' problems. But that sounds too mechanical. For one thing, we're talking about creative problems—this "work" feels more like play. For another, each problem is unique, and requires a fresh approach. The trick is, first, to determine what the problem is, and then to solve it in an innovative way.

Wise designers know that the first trick is sometimes as hard to perform as the second. Helping clients fully articulate their requirements is a skill that not every designer has mastered; it can demand the research and listening skills of a good investigative reporter, along with the patience of Job.

The second trick—solving the problem in an innovative way—can be even more difficult. It's easy for most designers to come up with something that merely looks pretty; in fact, that's often how younger designers approach their assignments. Seasoned professionals, however, try to push the envelope a little with each job: to find a way to make each design fresh and original. There are many ways to do this, from a novel use of type to an unexpected choice of imagery or format. The end result should be more interesting than a superbly executed design that follows all the rules—and is therefore too familiar. No one really looks at something seen a million times before. There are probably very few people, for example, who would really be able to remember a logo for a fire department if it included dalmatians—or maybe even the color red. The more unexpected and daring the solution, the greater the impact it will have.

The willingness to try something new is a hallmark of good designers at every stage of a project, from concept to final execution. The goal is always to produce design that is vibrant and alive, with something to say to an audience—and designers know they've succeeded if people want to keep looking at it. Further, designers must be sure they're saying the appropriate thing, using color, type, and the other elements of their craft to produce an appropriate emotional response in the viewer.

A good design is a solution so obvious that it's not obvious that it was designed. It appears natural and inevitable, as if there could be no other solution. It starts with a good idea and ends with good execution. Neither a good idea (vision without technique) nor good execution (technique without vision) alone is enough—in a good design, vision must harmoniously unite with technique.

And, of course, the finished design must please the client. But what about those times when the client wants the project done in corporate colors, let's say navy and gold, but is targeting teens? That's when responsible designers must ask the client to reconsider. On the other hand, responsible designers also must have the integrity to compromise between creating work that is aesthetically pleasing to the connoisseur and work that is marketable for the client. There may come a time when navy and gold are just the thing! Once the problem is clearly articulated, it's

time for some analysis. This is another stage when research skills come in handy: the client's history should be studied, and comparable materials surveyed. The object is to isolate something unique about the particular client and the particular job. Then comes a period of brainstorming, when creative freewheeling begins. At this point, smart designers temporarily forget the goal. They put everything aside and think freely, ignoring trends and preconceived notions. By pushing the envelope, and then pulling it back, the designer usually finds that he or she has come up with a crazy idea or two that might actually be worth trying.

Wise designers don't rely on software tricks to test ideas—if an idea is good, they know they should be able to get it across in something as simple as a thumbnail sketch. This doesn't mean, of course, that they don't revise their plans once a project is underway—like painters, they step back at regular intervals and ask themselves, do I want that shadow? Should I change this shape?

The finished product looks good and accomplishes the client's goals, preferably in an instant. Good design communicates effectively at as general a level as possible, giving viewers the essence of what's being communicated at a glance. Everything is in place—and only the wise designer needs to know how it got that way: through a collaborative client relationship, a willingness to try something new, a strong concept, and strong execution. All anyone else needs to know is that it looks great!

But intelligent designers share one more trait. They don't rest on their laurels, because they know that good design doesn't merely repeat the last good design. Instead, each project brings something new to life.

The Supon Design Group staff, left to right: Brent Almond, Jacques Coughlin, Andrew Berman, Jason Drumheller, Tom Klinedinst, Alexander Chang, Supon Phornirunlit (holding Pica the Wonder Dog), Sharisse Steber, Debbi Savitt, Wayne Kurie, Jake Lefebure, Andy Dolan, Khoi Vinh, Saundrea Cika, Greg Varner, Dujdao "Pum" Mek-aroonreung, Usha Rindani (holding Cricket), Richard Law, Colm Owens, Steve Delin.

Based in Washington, D.C., since its founding in 1988, Supon Design Group has grown rapidly into a world-class design power-house with almost 700 industry awards to its credit. Specializing in a wide spectrum of projects, SDG has divided into three busy divisions; the graphic studio alone lists clients ranging from small mom-and-pop shops and non-profit groups to multinational enterprises. SDG's international book division has many award-winning commercial arts titles to its credit, as well as several other visually stunning books, while the product division is dedicated to developing an extraordinary array of items, from software to innova-tive stationery packages. More than twenty designers and writers make up the Supon Design Group team, each with his or her own special skills and area of expertise.

A strong team orientation and lighthearted tone distinguish the SDG offices in downtown Washington, where visitors are greeted by the firm's mascots, Pica and Cricket, a miniature pomeranian and a papillon, respectively. Vibrant and playful objects dot the studio's walls and

shelves, keeping spirits bright. In the words of one SDG designer, "It's a fabulous atmosphere." The playful tone maintained by the Supon Design Group staff translates into good working relationships with clients. Noted for its exceptional service orientation and close client contact, SDG has inspired fierce loyalty among its clients. The firm's commitment to its customers, in turn, is demonstrated by its fair pricing and its proven track record at partnering with clients to develop innovative products—either for distribution through their own channels or for sale to trade vendors.

Typically, several designers will be involved in each SDG project at every level, from preliminary sketches to finished piece. This has two positive, interrelated consequences. First, the finished product will be richer and stronger, given the diversity of its "gene pool" (trust SDG to come up with a bioevolutionary theory of design). And second, the designers themselves are kept awake, interested, and sharp by the variety of projects they're able to tackle. Every member of the team contributes to a variety of projects in all three SDG specialties: the graphic studio, the product division, and the international book division.

Fortunately, the projects at Supon Design Group tend to be exciting and challenging. "We're doing what most designers are dying to do," enthuses one SDG team member. "Clients come to us for creativity, and not merely for production." Whether the need is for a magazine layout, a full-scale identity campaign, a simple ad—or anything else—the team at SDG is sure to satisfy the client's objective.

Supon Design Group is pleased to present some examples of our work to readers of this book. We hope you'll agree that these are, indeed, examples of wise design.

Web Site

Visiting Supon Design Group's web site is like visiting Supon Design Group. Included are a virtual tour through the studio, samples of recent work, and background information on the company and its key staff. The site's look was just redesigned to reflect the firm's colorful new identity. Loose, textural illustrations in a contemporary, but primitive, style coexist with subtle photographic images to portray the graphic diversity of Supon Design Group.

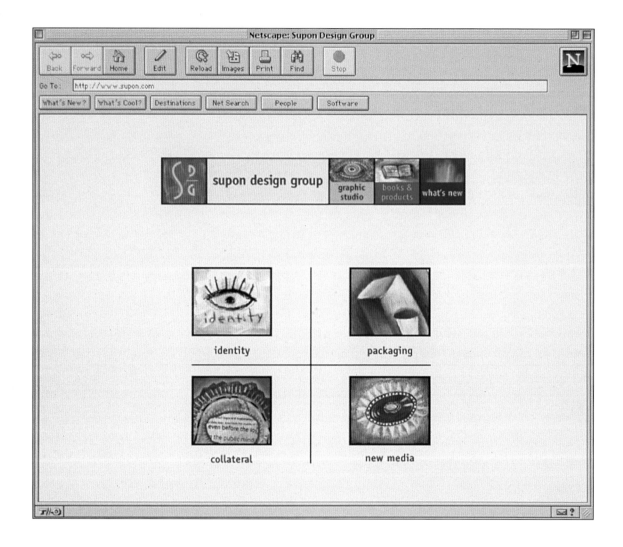

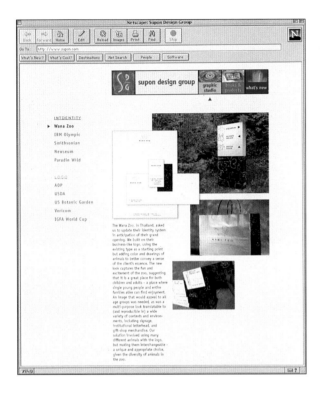

Unlike many of our recent web-site clients, NWDA already had a site running. Our challenge was to upgrade the existing site's graphics and make it easier to use. We chose a very clean and friendly design—one which would facilitate the site's role as an informational conduit between pharmaceutical manufacturers, pharmacists, and end users, i.e., patients.

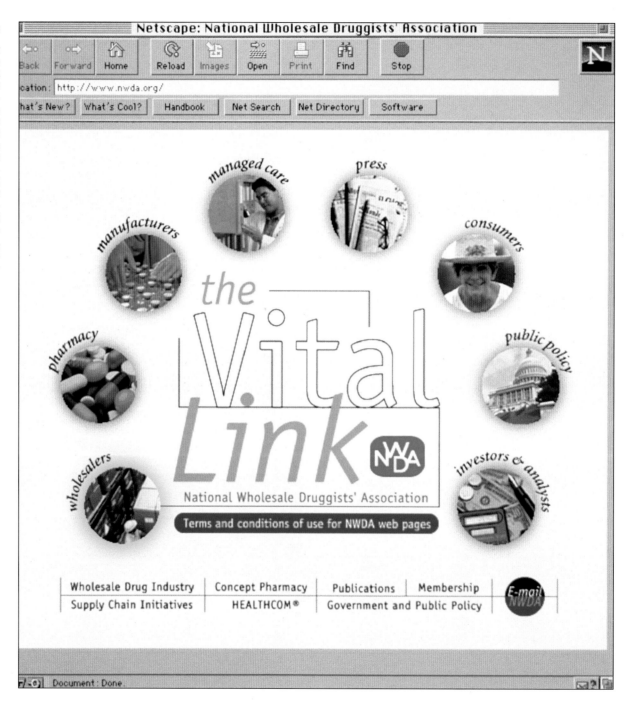

Web Site

The Museum of Junk is a Singaporean retail store which sells decorative accessories and collectibles—both antiques and reproductions. Its new web site has three primary sections which include information about the store, its products, and locations. The design of the site is festive, with bright colors permeating every screen graphic. An enlarged version of the museum's logo is used as a jacquard-like background behind all graphics. This added texture suggests the rich and luxurious quality of many of the store's products.

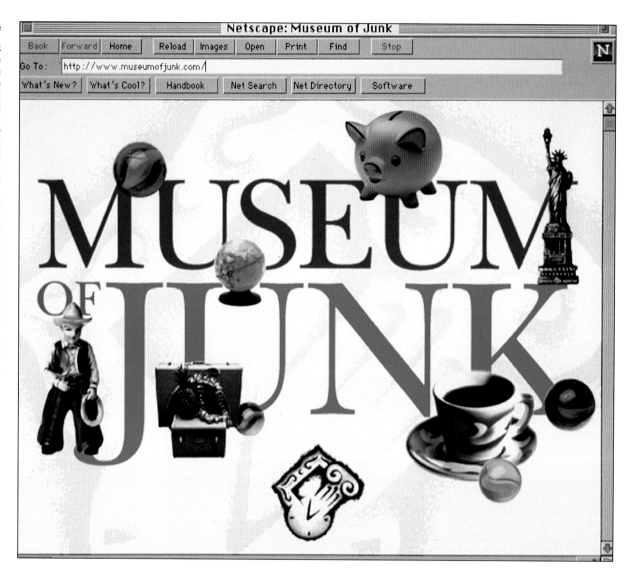

**Logo and
Packaging**

In order to position
itself ahead of the
Internet curve,
Prodigy wanted a
more contemporary
design. The
redesigned logo
retains the familiar
star, but updates it
and gives it new
typography. To
further advance the
new look, the
revised star became
the focus of the
packaging's multi-
color graphics.

NetFinity Brochures

NetFinity is one of IBM's new systems-management software programs. These two brochures—one targeting end users and the other corporate partners—emphasize the product's many benefits. Photographic images are layered and juxtaposed throughout to suggest connectivity and integration between elements. The "Partners" brochure takes this concept a step further: Images form puzzle pieces which fit together to illustrate how NetFinity enables systems to network together.

Marketing Kit

Iridium's hand-held telephones allow subscribers to communicate with anyone in the world using the most up-to-date technology. Its marketing pieces emphasize this capability with diagrams and copy describing the product's global reach. The covers contain striking graphics of a segmented sphere—at once suggestive of the Earth, communications, and high technology. To further promote Iridium's international coverage, the term "personal global communications" is superimposed on the sphere in a handful of languages on the inside pockets of the portfolio.

Owner's Manual

Digital Ink represents The Washington Post's initial entry into online newspapers. Its primary niche is the local Washington, D.C. market. Exemplified here by the Owner's Manual, the colorful marketing identity suggests the boldness of concept and technical expertise of the subscription service.

Marketing Kit

Its name often shortened to CASI, this organization provides computer-systems networking solutions to corporate clients. Its marketing kit is in the form of a folder with several different template sheets inside which can be customized as necessary. This piece was designed utilizing the client's preexisting logo—building blocks in the three primary colors, red, blue, and yellow. The kit's design plays these up, creating a graphic metaphor for CASI's "object-oriented" software, the building blocks of more complex computer programs.

FEW INITIATIVES CAN HAVE AS POSITIVE AN IMPACT ON PUBLIC RELATIONS AS OLYMPIC GAMES SPONSORSHIP. OUR STRATEGY FOR CREATING IBM'S OLYMPIC LOOK WAS TO PROMOTE BOTH IBM'S SPONSORSHIP OF THE OLYMPICS AND THE GAMES THEMSELVES. THE HORIZONTAL BLUE STRIPES FROM ITS CORPORATE LOGO IMMEDIATELY AND FORCEFULLY CALL IBM TO MIND, WHILE IMAGES SUCH AS THE CAULDRON, RINGS, AND ATHLETES IN MOTION OBVIOUSLY SUGGEST THE GAMES. OUR APPROACH WAS TO BLEND THESE ELEMENTS AS SMOOTHLY AND COMPLETELY AS POSSIBLE, SELLING IBM'S PARTICIPATION IN THE GAMES MORE THAN ITS PRODUCTS. JUST AS ITS BLUE STRIPES ARE INTEGRATED INTO THE DESIGN, IBM IS REFLECTED AS AN INTEGRAL PART OF THE GAMES. APPLIED TO EVERYTHING FROM T-SHIRTS AND WARM-UP JACKETS TO LUGGAGE TAGS, COFFEE MUGS, MOUSEPADS AND OTHER OFFICE ACCESSORIES, IBM'S LOOK OF THE GAMES HELPED FOSTER A SPIRIT OF PRIDE BOTH INSIDE AND OUTSIDE THE CORPORATE WALLS.

**Olympic
Sponsorship
Identity**

Full-spectrum
illustrations of
Olympic athletes
were layered
amongst IBM's
quintessential blue
stripes to create the
identity for the
corporation's
sponsorship of the
1996 Centennial
Games in Atlanta.
IBM's "look of the
Games" was applied
to dozens of items,
including billboards,
posters, truck sides,
hats, T-shirts, and
visors—many with
multi-sport versions.

Olympic Sponsorship Identity

In all, approximately 30 different sports icons were created as part of the identity of IBM's Olympic sponsorship. These were used in many different ways including a website application.

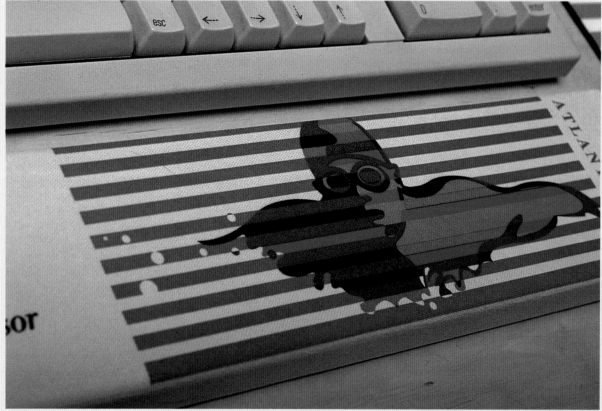

Olympic Sponsorship Identity

The Design Guide outlined the graphics standards for IBM's 1996 Olympic sponsorship identity. Outside vendors and manufacturers used these guidelines along with furnished art on disk for the production of dozens of items. Among these were the caps, Hosting Program, and mugs shown at right.

**Proposed Olympic
Sponsorship
Identity**

A wide range of
applications formed
the proposed identity
for Coca-Cola's 1996
Atlanta Olympic
Games sponsorship.
Among them were
T-shirts, posters,
billboards, truck
panels, shopping
bags, and sports
bottles. Several full
campaigns were
designed, with each
targeting a specific
market niche. The
familiar slogan
"Always Coca-Cola,"
for instance, became
"*Siempre* Coca-Cola
in a campaign for
young Hispanics.

Asia '95 T-shirts

This pair of T-shirts plus many more were designed to promote cooperation among the Asian countries through international sporting events. Graphics are bold and colorful, the style of choice for effective T-shirt merchandising.

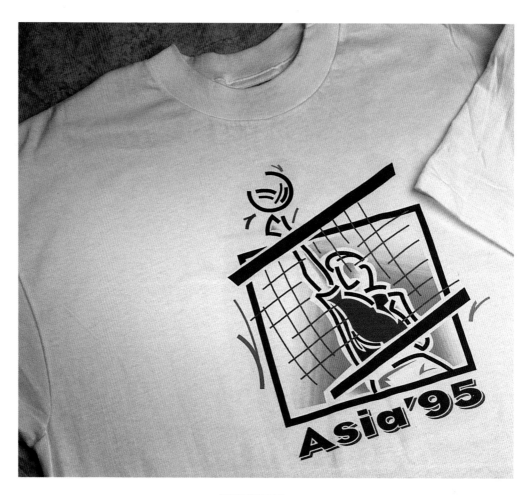

Athletic Sock Packaging

A series of several illustrations depicting different sports cover the packaging bands of this line of athletic socks. Weightlifting, track and field, and racquetball are each shown in a high-energy style of illustration. Wearhouse, a young athletic-wear company found this two-color packaging very economical to print.

Centennial Olympics T-shirts

Champion Sportswear was an official sponsor of Atlanta's 1996 Centennial Olympic Games. These are but two of the hundreds of T-shirts which were designed to promote the clothing line's unique affiliation with the Olympics. Many contain strong, immediately recognizable icons or illustrations of athletes in the thrill of competition; others celebrate the one-hundredth anniversary of the Modern Olympic Games.

**Atlanta Olympics
T-shirts**

Scores of T-shirt
designs were
created—each por-
traying the excite-
ment of Atlanta's
1996 Centennial
Olympic Games.
Designs varied
greatly, with some
promoting the
Atlanta city venue,
others emphasizing
specific sports, and
still others portray-
ing the grandeur of
the Olympics and the
100-year anniversary
of the Modern Games.

Season-Ticket Set

A full-color illustration blankets this set of season tickets to Washington, D.C.'s major-league soccer games. Its somewhat subdued, pastel palette is unexpected; bold colors in bright hues would be the natural choice for such high-visibility sports graphics.

World Cup Soccer Dossier

This brochure targets potential, high-dollar corporate sponsors of the next World Cup Soccer tournament to be held in France in 1998. Vibrant, full-color photos matchside demonstrate the huge international exposure enjoyed by past corporate sponsors: World Cup Soccer garners the largest television audience of any sporting event in the world.

WorldCup
USA**94**

DOSSIER

SEPTEMBER 1, 1992

"Name the Mascot" promotion is launched in the U.S. by
Marketing on behalf of the Official Sponsors. The public is ask
vote to name the 1994 World Cup mascot.

ISL Marketing's Chairman o
on players with Dr. Henry A.
World Cup USA 1994's Boar

IN THE 1800S, WHEN BRITISH CITIZEN JAMES SMITHSON WILLED HIS FORTUNE TO THE UNITED STATES GOVERNMENT FOR THE CREATION OF A MUSEUM, EVEN HE PROBABLY COULD NOT HAVE ENVISIONED ITS MODERN SCOPE. INSPIRED BY THEIR APPRECIATION OF PRODUCTS AND PACKAGING WE HAD PREVIOUSLY DESIGNED FOR SMITHSONIAN GIFT SHOPS, THE DESIGNERS OF THE SMITHSONIAN INSTITUTION'S 150TH ANNIVERSARY TRAVELING EXHIBITION ASKED US TO DEVELOP A LOOK FOR THEIR SESQUICENTENNIAL PRINTED MATERIALS. WE ADAPTED THE FAMILIAR SMITHSONIAN SUNBURST ICON, SPLITTING IT INTO FOUR PARTS: IN ONE QUADRANT, WE REPRESENTED THE ORIGINAL ICON, WHILE USING THE OTHERS TO ILLUSTRATE THE THREE EXHIBIT THEMES—DISCOVERING, IMAGINING, AND REMEMBERING—PHOTOGRAPHICALLY. OUR LOOK WAS APPLIED TO THE EXHIBIT ITSELF, ON ENTRANCES TO EACH OF THE THREE THEME AREAS. WORKING WITH THE SMITHSONIAN CREATIVE TEAM, WE ALSO DEVELOPED A SIGNAGE SYSTEM FOR THE EXHIBIT, UTILIZING PHOTOGRAPHIC AND POSTERIZED IMAGES.

REMEMBERING

America's Smithsonian Identity

America's Smithsonian is the name of the traveling exhibition commemorating the Smithsonian Institution's 150th anniversary and contains a selection of the museums' most treasured objects. With "Discovering, Imagining, Remembering" its theme, the images used encourage people to ponder the cultural, historical, and physical importance of each item. On some pieces, combinations of artifacts form the familiar Smithsonian sunburst.

America's Smithsonian Identity

In several cities to which the America's Smithsonian exhibition traveled, bilingual signage was created. The sunburst design of these on-site murals was also used on the press kit's pocket folder and stationery system.

America's Smithsonian Identity

A graphics standards manual, which included a full set of art on disk, was developed for use by outside vendors for the production and manufacture of dozens of items. Among these were the tote and shopping bags shown here.

**Affiliate
Marketing Kit**

With an already
strong presence in
the cable television
industry, BET sought
to expand its affiliate
base, strengthen
existing markets,
and broaden ad
sales. The resulting
kit design includes a
myriad of active
images that promote
the channel's broad
programming. A
single, coordinated
design included a
demo tape, pocket
folder, and various
letterheads and
brochures.

BET on Jazz Brochure

Black Entertainment Television's second channel is BET on Jazz. Since its audience is somewhat older and more affluent than BET's general demographics, the design of its brochure is a simpler and more conservative version of the affiliate marketing brochure shown on the facing page. The deep colors and powerful imagery, however, remain.

"I think (BET On Jazz) is a great idea and it can have a great impact on music. I hope that BET can expose people to what jazz is through educational programs and provide a forum for young musicians to play and be seen by people around the country playing real jazz music. I hope that BET can help to differentiate and distinguish what makes this art form different from other art forms."

Wynton Marsalis, renowned jazz performer, composer and educator

**Discovery Asia
Identity**

In recent years, the
Discovery Channel
has made great
inroads into inter-
national markets. A
pocket folder and
letterhead package
displays Discovery
International's
new identity.
Photographic images
from around the
world are combined
with navigational
lines of latitude and
longitude to suggest
the company's new
global reach.

Know-TV Identity

Know-TV is a series of workshops developed by The Learning Channel to promote responsible television viewing. The identity's boldly illustrated graphics depict an eye which, at second glance, becomes a full human figure. Microphones, cameras, and other television-related icons are printed in a tinted varnish to add interest to the background. Included among the educational materials are a program binder, video casette, and pocket folder.

Corporate Brochure

ISL Marketing is an organization which manages and promotes international sporting events worldwide. To portray the company's reach, the wire-bound brochure and its accompanying inserts feature photographs of athletes from sports as diverse as skiing, track and field, and soccer. Throughout its colorful pages, the excitement of international competition is palpable.

**TV Europe
Marketing Brochure**

Targeting larger communications firms for a potential joint venture, this brochure presents TV Europe, a new cable television channel which brings European programming to America. The brochure's split-image cover graphically portrays this concept: The TV Europe logo straddles several well known landmarks on both sides of the Atlantic. Inside, the unique characteristics and strong market potential of the channel are clearly described and illustrated.

**18th Annual BDA
Design Awards
Call for Entries**

BDA's annual awards event would be held in Los Angeles, so a whimsical, multi-hued, "Hollywood" look was suggested for its Call for Entries. The cover's illustrative style was carried through on the inside to include additional personages as well as lighthearted borders and textures. The look purposely steered clear of the trendy "street" look so overused in media design today.

**International Logos
& Trademarks III
Call for Entries**

To succeed in encouraging designers to submit their work to a graphics competition, a call for entries must be striking. And because the intended market is other designers, its look can be more "cutting edge" or avant-garde than that of other business-to-business marketing pieces. The combination of typography and imagery of this call for entries approaches the limits but is careful not to exceed them.

2020 Vision
Campaign

To facilitate the
feeding of the world,
the prevention of
poverty, and the
protection of the
Earth is the mission
of IFPRI, the Inter-
national Food Policy
Research Institute.
Such lofty organiza-
tional goals could
easily seem imper-
sonal or bureaucratic.
To counter this, a
warm and earthy
illustrative style
quickly became the
common identity for
each of IFPRI's 2020
Vision print commu-
nications pieces.
These include the
program's Executive
Summary, Resources
Catalog, and promo-
tional poster.
Recycled stock in a
natural, speckled
color cinches the
environmental look.

FEEDING THE WORLD ❦ PREVENTING POVERTY / PROTECTING THE EARTH

Annual Report

The cover's montage of similarly toned photographs against a crisp, white background foretells this corporation's biotechnological bent. The interior's easy-to-follow, two-color design reflects that of the cover—very clean with lots of white space.

Housing Reports

The covers of these reports for Fannie Mae feature snapshots of many of the families and individuals who have benefited from the organization's programs which make housing available and affordable to people of all income levels. Their scrapbook format personalizes the services offered and presents the company as a wholesome, accessible, and all-American partner.

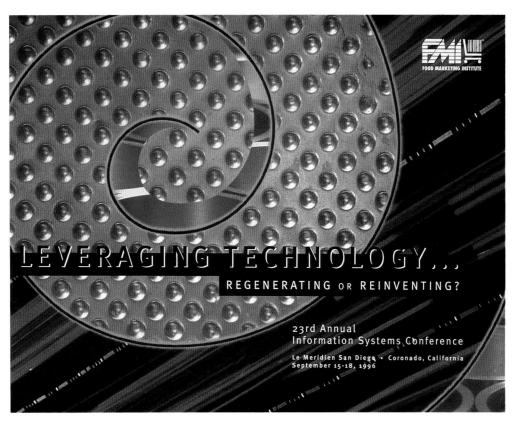

Information Systems Conference Promotions

Instead of conducting a single, all-encompassing annual meeting like many trade associations, FMI sponsors as series of specialized events, each targeting a specific market or industry segment. These brochures promote FMI's 22nd and 23rd Annual Information Systems Conferences. Photo collages include computers and other high-tech elements which instantly appeal to the intended audience.

ASID Report

The American
Society of Interior
Designers' monthly
magazine was in
need of a new look.
In addition to
redesigning the pub-
lication, a full set of
graphic standards
for future editions
was created. This
new, more contem-
porary guise is
befitting an industry
whose own mission
is effective design
with strong
aesthetics.

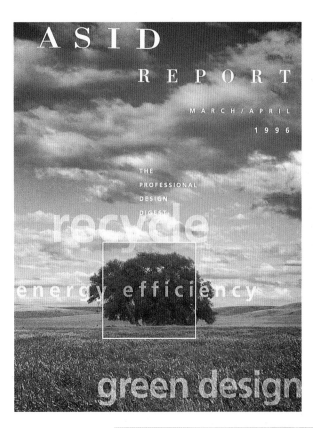

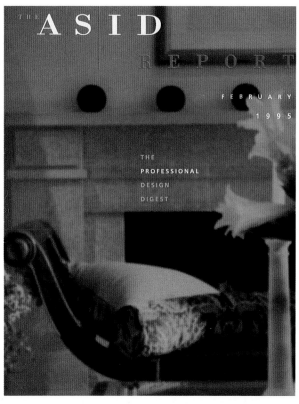

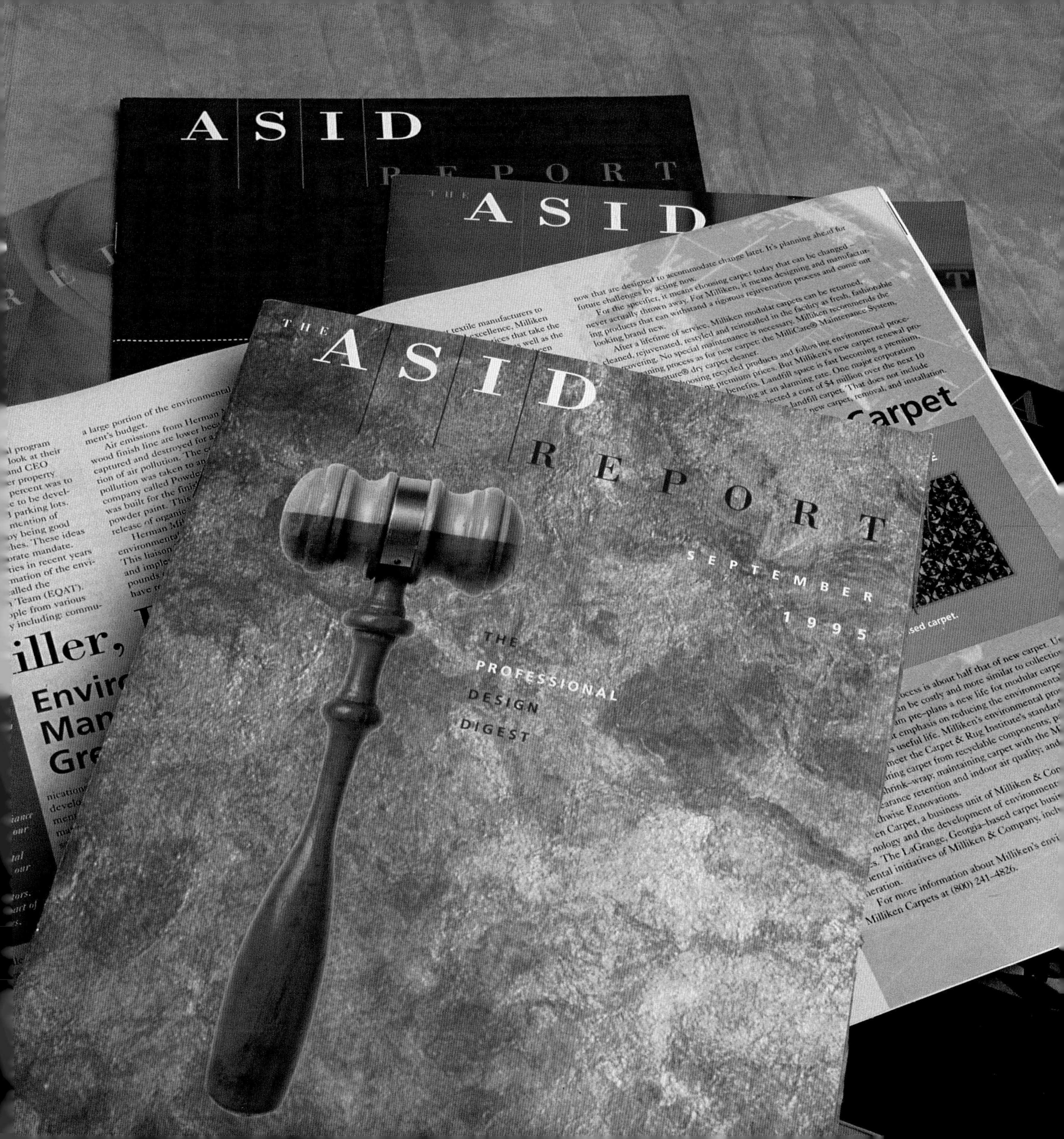

ASID

THE ASID

THE ASID

REPORT

SEPTEMBER 1995

THE PROFESSIONAL DESIGN DIGEST

Marketing Brochure

The Progressive Life Center is a psychiatric facility which helps individuals through difficult relationships or periods in their lives. To reflect the center's predominately African-American clientele, illustrative art suggestive of African kente cloth bedecks the brochure's cover and frames each page of interior text. Rich, inviting colors combined with photos of many of the center's programs and personnel portray a culture of warmth, accessibility, and professionalism.

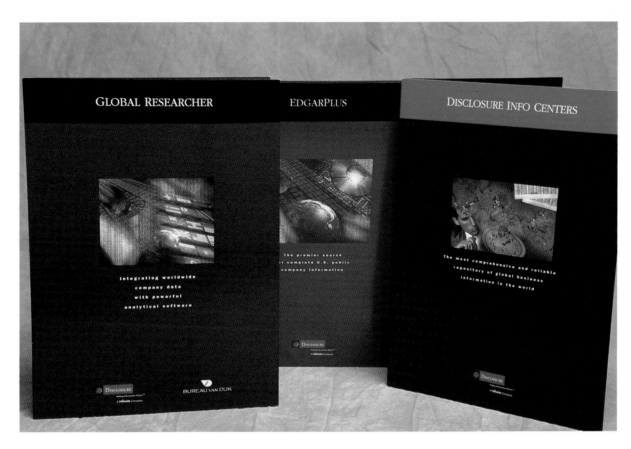

Marketing Brochures

A trio of capability brochures describes the range of services offered by Disclosure, the nation's leading provider of data on public companies worldwide. Each embraces a tri-fold format and contains a single interior pocket. Their coordinated design — high-tech and active — imparts a real-time urgency to the company's products.

RECRUITMENT MATERIALS FOR SCHOOLS SUCH AS THE GEORGE WASHINGTON UNIVERSITY MUST BE INCREASINGLY SOPHISTICATED FOR TODAY'S COMPETITIVE MARKET. WELL BEFORE BEGINNING THEIR SENIOR YEAR OF HIGH SCHOOL, PROSPECTIVE CANDIDATES FOR ADMISSION ARE TARGETED BY AN OVERALL MARKETING CAMPAIGN, INCLUDING PRINT MEDIA, VIDEOS, AND INTERACTIVE MULTIMEDIA. OUR STRATEGY FOR GW WAS TO DESIGN COLORFUL AND ENERGETIC MATERIALS WHICH WOULD APPEAL TO THE YOUNG AUDIENCE WHO HAD GROWN UP WITH MTV, THE EVOLUTION OF COMPUTERS AND THE INFORMATION SUPERHIGHWAY, AND WHO WERE ACCUSTOMED TO CONSTANTLY CHANGING VISUAL STIMULI. AT THE SAME TIME, OUR GENEROUS LAYOUT OF TEXT AND PALATABLE "BITES" OF INFORMATION WERE MEANT TO APPEAL TO THE SECONDARY MARKETS REPRESENTED BY PARENTS AND HIGH SCHOOL COUNSELORS. WE HIGHLIGHT GW'S LOCATION IN THE NATION'S CAPITAL AND ITS ABILITY TO OFFER STUDENTS A HIGH LEVEL OF ACCESS TO MAJOR FIGURES ON THE NATIONAL AND INTERNATIONAL SCENE.

GW Viewbook

The GW Viewbook is sent to high-school seniors who've requested information about the University. Its minimalist cover contrasts greatly with the active interior spreads at right. It's designed to attract the more sophisticated of those who've grown up with interactive television, computer games, and MTV. Photos, type, and graphics wow the reader; headlines compete for attention; and the aggressive, oversized format doesn't hold back. Its theme, "You will...," raises expectations high—then delivers. Something really does happen here.

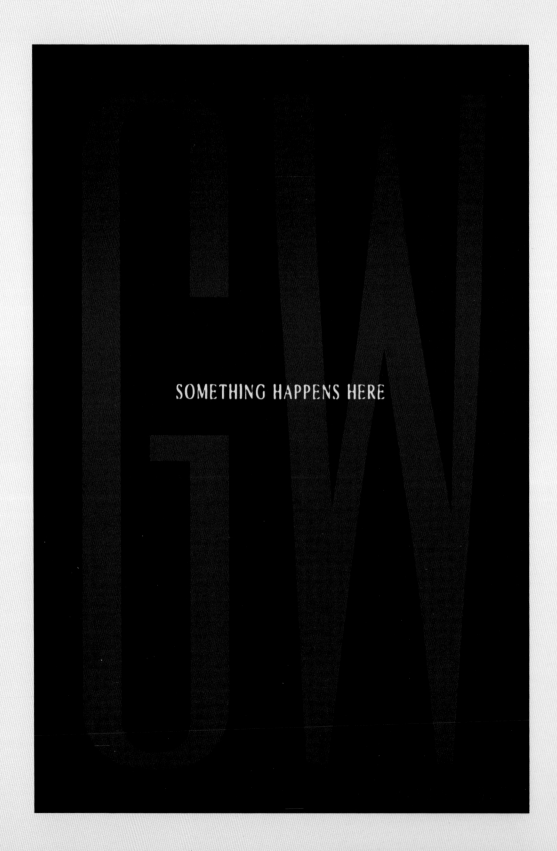

SOMETHING HAPPENS HERE

GW Viewbox

A previous year's
Viewbook was
housed in a box
containing a video,
buttons, and
individual school
and departmental
brochures. The
book's no-holds-
barred graphics
were carried
through to form
a package with
lots of punch.

you will design robotic co...

you will rise to numerous intellectual challenges.

you will measure the speed of light.

you will describe the origin and evolution of the universe.

you will explore forces of... driving busin... the 21st c...

you will encounter advisors who add depth and relevance to your studies.

Search Piece

This engaging promotion is sent to high-school sophomores who've just begun thinking about college. With a friendly look and manner, it profiles the University and its students. It provides just enough information to pique the students' interest, and leaves them wanting to know more.

Recruitment Promotion

With photos of current students and faculty, this accordion-fold brochure depicts the richness and diversity of intellectual life at GW. As each panel is unfolded, the breadth of possibilities that a GW education offers becomes clearer and clearer and clearer....

Colonial Inauguration Program

This innovative brochure introduces incoming students—the Class of 2000—to Colonial Inauguration, the University's summer orientation program. With images of past presidential campaigns and the atomic space age, its design bridges the gap between past and present, nostalgic and futuristic. The kicker is the cover: it's designed to be viewed through 3-D glasses.

Club Iowa Soft Drink Packaging

Sassy & Strawberry and Lemon Bite are just two flavors in Club Iowa's line of soft drinks targeting Asian teens and young adults. Because of the current popularity of America's pop culture abroad, the Thailand-based Grand Palace Foods International wanted an American name and image. The brand's new, bold graphics and bright colors appeal to this young market.

Gobéy Soy Sauce Packaging

A line of light, regular, and thick soy sauces, Gobéy is sold in upscale gourmet shops. Its packaging design reflects this market with its high-style label and bottle shape.

Product Identity

These fun, colorful, high-energy graphics will wake you up in the morning—even without the caffeine. They're part of a line of coffee-related accessories for sale at neighborhood coffee shops in Thailand.

Paradise Rice Wine Packaging

The simply elegant design of the label harmonizes with the graceful curves of this rice wine's bottle. Its minimalist style reflects the wine's Asian, especially Japanese, origins.

EAS

$1.75

MANGO

AMARETTO

EARL GREY

SPEARMINT

DEJARRLING

ORANGE PEKOE

VANILLA ALMOND

STRAWBERRIES & CREAM

& lemon add .50]

DESSERTS

$3.50

COCONUT CAKE w/LEMON FILLING

FUDGE POUND CAKE w/CREAM

LEMON MUFFINS

RUM CAKE

MUFFINS

COOKIE

ARES

AKE

TE

$2.25

flavored

Tea- and Coffeeshop Packaging and Identity

Steep Thoughts is the witty name for a combination bookstore/tea- and coffeeshop. The soft, ethereal borders of the graphic images throughout the identity suggest the haze created by steaming coffee or tea as well as the constantly changing cast of characters in the shop. Underlying the illustrations are subtle passages of text which bridge the gap between the literary and the consumable— thereby fulfilling the shop's high concept.

"Crew" Jacket

As an end-of-the year "thank you," each staff member of Supon Design Group received a leather jacket. The theme "Supon Design Crew" was selected to emphasize teamwork amongst the firm's employees.

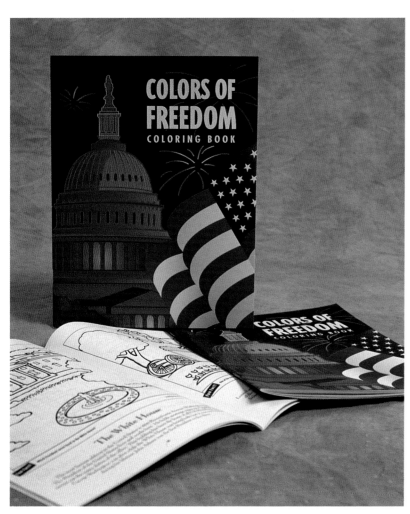

Colors of Freedom Coloring Book

A spin-off of the popular *Our Nation's Capital in 3-D*, this coloring book involves children even further in America's government and history. Well known Washington, D.C., landmarks are included in black outline format, ready for kids to color. Should the White House remain white? Or be colored blue, green, or polka dot? Let the kids decide.

Our Nation's Capital in 3-D

With 3-D images of the Capitol, White House, Smithsonian Castle, and more, this book helps children imagine they've gone on a family vacation to Washington, D.C. They delight in putting on the 3-D glasses—housed in a pocket on the book's back cover— and viewing each of the buildings, museums, or monuments that make our city so striking

What's in a Number?

Do the letters of your name or the numbers of your birth date hold secrets to your personality? This fun-filled, novelty book says they can. And it's easy to find out how. Delightful illustrations, fanciful calligraphy, and a light-hearted design that doesn't take itself too seriously distinguish this book from others in its genre. Tabs, wheels, and windows make the book fun and interactive.

BY GEORGE PIERSON

Sneaky Questions

Sneaky Questions was one of Supon Design Group's first forays into general-interest, novelty titles. With the answers to innocuous questions such as "What's your favorite animal?," the reader can build a personality profile of his or her friends or family members. Creative use of color and an unusual mixing of illustrations and photographs distinguish this book.

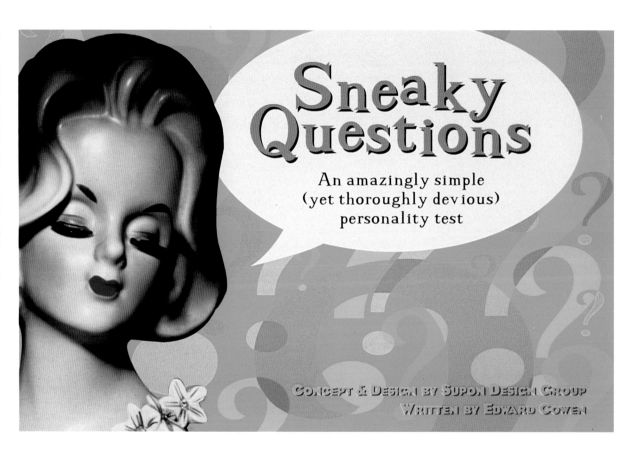

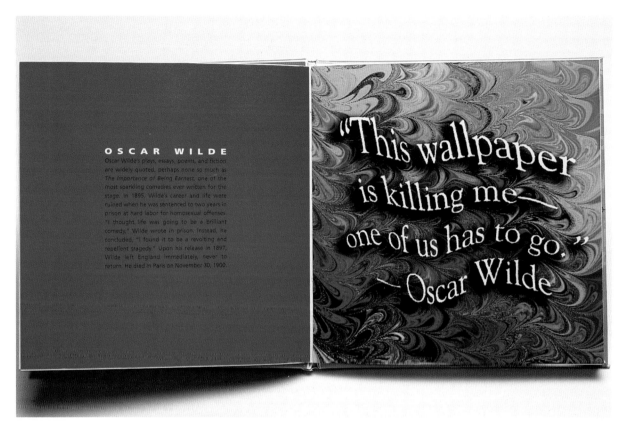

OSCAR WILDE

Oscar Wilde's plays, essays, poems, and fiction are widely quoted, perhaps none so much as *The Importance of Being Earnest*, one of the most sparkling comedies ever written for the stage. In 1895, Wilde's career and life were ruined when he was sentenced to two years in prison at hard labor for homosexual offenses. "I thought life was going to be a brilliant comedy," Wilde wrote in prison. Instead, he concluded, "I found it to be a revolting and repellent tragedy." Upon his release in 1897, Wilde left England immediately, never to return. He died in Paris on November 30, 1900.

***Last Word on
Last Words***

Believe it or not: Some people can be witty even on their deathbed. This booklet features approximately 20 such statements spoken by famous (or infamous) personages before expiring. Each is given a full spread, with the person's name and short biography on the left page and the quote brought to life in full-color illustration on the right. Not the least bit morbid, this booklet pays tribute to icons of our culture and the verbal chestnuts that made them so.

MAKING TRACKS TO CARE FOR OUR ENVIRONMENT

Animal Tracks®

Education Program of the National Wildlife Federation®

Animal Tracks

River Otte

River otters look like they are built for swimming. Their long bodies cut through the water, and their short legs and webbed feet propel them. They swim fast, up to seven miles an hour. That's fast! Even world-only swim a little more than five miles an hour. two species of otters in the United States: sea otters. Sea otters live in the ocean and nd. River otters make their dens on land where they catch fresh fish to eat a

ots of water. They build their important that the water there.

ook for their tracks marks that sho grass,

and all wo we'll

nking, swim

watering our

Water Conservation

River Otter

River otters look like they are built for swimming. Their long bodies cut through the water, and their short legs and webbed feet propel them. They swim fast, up to seven miles an hour. That's fast! Even world-class athletes only swim a little more than five miles an hour.

There are two species of otters in the United States: sea otters and river otters. Sea otters live in the ocean and rarely come on land. River otters make their dens on land, but live near water, where they catch fresh fish to eat and feed their young.

River otters need lots of water. They build their dens near rivers or lakes. It's important that the water be clean in order for otters to survive there.

If otters live near you, look for their tracks. You might see paw prints, or long, smooth marks that show where they slide in snow, mud or along grass.

A river otter, like you and all other living things, needs a clean and healthy world. Follow the otter's tracks to find out how you can conserve water so we'll always have enough for drinking, swimming or watering our plants.

24 Animal Tracks Water Conservation 25

Squirrel

What animal do you see the most in your backyard? It might be a tree squirrel, easy to spot racing up tree trunks, leaping across fenceposts and scurrying over roof tops. Squirrels are lightning-fast and very acrobatic, and that helps them live in the woods, in neighborhoods or even in the busiest cities.

We call them tree squirrels (gray squirrels, red squirrels or flying squirrels) because they make their nests in trees. Nature equips them for that kind of life.

Their claws are sharp, which helps them grasp tree branches. Their bushy tails keep them balanced. Their eyes are on the sides of their head, which helps them spot animals sneaking up on them.

Some animals can live in only one kind of habitat, or home. A whale can live only in salt water; a mountain goat can never live in a city. But squirrels are adaptable as long as they can find the food they need and can build a nest above the ground.

A squirrel, like you and all other living things, needs a clean and healthy world. Follow the squirrel's tracks to find out how you can keep your backyard healthy for you, other people, pets and wildlife.

yummy

home sweet home

Animal Tracks Backyard Wildlife 9

Animal Tracks

Subtitled *Making Tracks to Care for Our Environment*, this full-color, illustrated book is part of the National Wildlife Federation's Conservation Education Program. Each section begins with an illustration of an animal and information about it which includes how the animal can be identified by its tracks. The text then segues into a series of activities and exercises which teach children in grades 4 – 6 to care for their environment. Throughout, head lines, numbers, sidebars, and illustrations are brightly colored. The animal illustrations are at once realistic and friendly.

THE UNITED STATES POSTAL SERVICE GOES EVERY-WHERE, AND IS CONSTANTLY IN THE PUBLIC EYE; IN LIGHT OF THIS WIDE DISTRIBUTION, THEIR PRODUCTS NEED TO BE ESPECIALLY USER-FRIENDLY AND ACCESSIBLE. A STEADY STREAM OF NEW COMMEMORATIVE STAMPS (HONORING GEORGIA O'KEEFFE, FOR EXAMPLE, OR MARILYN MONROE, OR AMERICAN INDIAN DANCES, TO LIST JUST A FEW RECENT ISSUES) CREATES A SEEMINGLY INEXHAUSTIBLE NEED FOR EXCITING SOUVENIR PRODUCTS WITH EYE-CATCHING DESIGN AND LIVELY COPY. USING THE SUBJECTS SHOWN ON THE STAMPS AS STYLISTIC AND CONCEPTUAL STARTING POINTS, WE HAVE CREATED MANY SUCH PRODUCTS, OFTEN WITH ELEMENTS SUCH AS DIE-CUTS AND FOLD-OUTS ADDED TO GIVE THEM A SPECIAL FLAIR. BOLD GRAPHICS, VIVID COLORS AND INNOVATIVE LAYOUTS COMBINE TO REFLECT THE EXCITEMENT AND UNIQUENESS OF THE POSTAL SERVICE'S NEW GENERATION OF POSTAGE STAMPS, DISTINGUISHED BY A RANGE OF SUBJECT MATTER SO BROAD THAT EACH NEW PROJECT IS GUARANTEED TO BRING ITS OWN PARTICULAR CHALLENGES AND REWARDS.

Legends of the Silent Screen

Rudolf Valentino, Buster Keaton, Charlie Chaplin, and Clara Bow are among the ten stars from yesteryear whose talent and celebrity are honored by a set of commemorative stamps issued by the United States Postal Service. Richly illustrated with hundreds of photos, the corresponding book, *Legends of the Silent Screen*, tells of an era when Hollywood really was that shining city on the hill. Affixed to the inside of this book is a genuine block of all ten postage stamps, each illustrated by the well-known cartoonist Al Hirschfeld.

American Comic Classics

To celebrate the 100th anniversary of the comic strip, the United States Postal Service issued a set of commemorative stamps featuring 20 of the most beloved characters from comics' first 50 years. The pages of this book look like they were torn right from the comics. Full-color cartoons of each character—Blondie, Flash Gordon, Little Orphan Annie, and others—are interspersed with information about the strips and their artists. A block of all 20 commemorative stamps is mounted on the inside of the book, making this a true collector's item.

U.S.P.S. Pro-Cycling Team Poster

A series of posters was designed for the Pro-Cycling Team of the United States Postal Service. Each promoted a different city's race and featured very active illustrations of cyclists superimposed onto background images specific to each city. Affixed to each poster was a genuine U.S. postage stamp cancelled on the day of the race. Some of the posters were signed by team members, making the posters all the more collectible.

Commemorative Stamp Souvenirs

As illustrated by these very diverse projects, souvenirs for the United States Postal Service can take on most any format. Each houses a single stamp or stamp set commemorating a particular person, culture, or event with a first-day-of-issue cancellation. Typically, a brief history about the stamps and their subjects is included.

(clockwise from top left)

Civil War Stamps Souvenir

Native American Dances Stamps Souvenir

Marathon Stamp Souvenir

(opposite page)

Georgia O'Keefe Stamp Souvenir

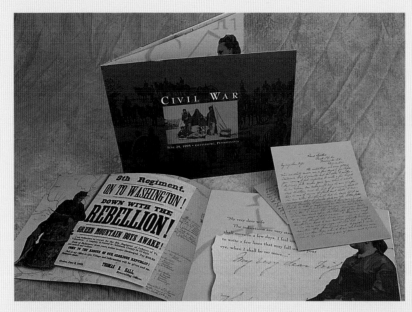

G

Georgia O'Keeffe's

earliest memory of her childhood in Wisconsin

was of the play of light on a quilt. She

years later, one of

modern artists. In a

O'Keeffe painted

nhattan

d in New

part of la

an

ch

O R G I A

K E E

FIRST DAY SOUVENIR

Nobody

really – it is so

d t

Georgia O'Keeffe

32 usa

GEORGIA O'KEEFFE FIRST DAY SOUVENIR

(clockwise from top left)

Marilyn Monroe Stamp Souvenir

Jazz Musicians Stamps Souvenir

James Dean Stamp Souvenir

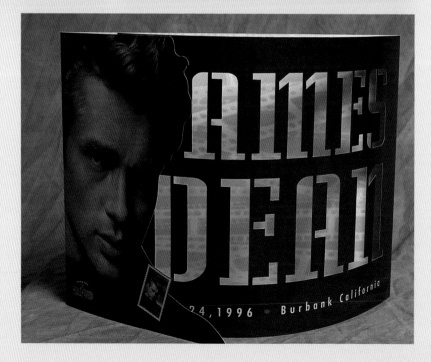

Centennial Olympic Games Postal Card Book and Stamps Souvenir

These two projects were created in time for the Centennial Modern Olympic Games in Atlanta. Twenty ready-to-mail, perforated postal cards are bound into a booklet (top). Each features a different full-bleed rendering of the illustrations of athletes which appear on the twenty U.S. postage stamps honoring these Olympians. With photographs of highlights from the past 100 years, the Stamps Souvenir (bottom) is a historic retrospect of the Modern Games.

(clockwise from top left)

Adventist HealthCare
Hospital consortium

Charles Button Company
Button manufacturer

Ulman Paper Bag Company
Paper-bag manufacturer

Harris Chair Company
Chair manufacturer

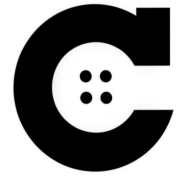

Logo and Identity

This top-of-the-line sail manufacturer had just changed its name to better reflect its positioning as a designer and fabricator of competitive, technologically-oriented sails. Its logo and identity complement the new, bolder name. The prominent "Q" is instantly recognizable as sails whip by in the height of competition.

Logo and Identity

The letterforms "C" and "K" which comprise this logo emphasize the personal attention given projects by partners Claydon and Klein. Since their business is conceiving and implementing innovative marketing solutions, the hand-rendered letterforms suggest creativity on a level that a stock-font treatment could not.

2020 Vision Stationery

2020 Vision is a program of IFPRI whose objective it is to eliminate hunger and malnutrition by the year 2020. The program's identity pairs the prominent "2020" with a more subtle image of a crescent moon to suggest the "eclipsing" of these all-too-prevalent— but preventable— conditions.

Logo and Identity

The Redmon Group develops interactive, multimedia software products for entertainment and educational purposes. The logo is comprised of an "R" casting a shadow to form the letter "G." Because of its affinity for science fiction, the client appreciated the hint of the futuristic in the look of the mark.

Logo and Identity

The full-color report covers and letterhead shown here each prominently display the MetaQuest logo. The interlocking color bars of both the mark and its applications suggest the varied services which this multimedia company offers.

Logo and Identity

TeleworX provides mapping software products and engineering consulting services for the wireless telecommunications industry. The names of each of TeleworX's products either begin or end with the letter "X."

The corporation's logo continues this practice—a bold, red "X" differentiates it from the competition. A yellow "O" and red-and-yellow swash suggest dynamism and give additional visual interest. To accentuate the logo, all other typography in the stationery package is black, set against a clean, white background.

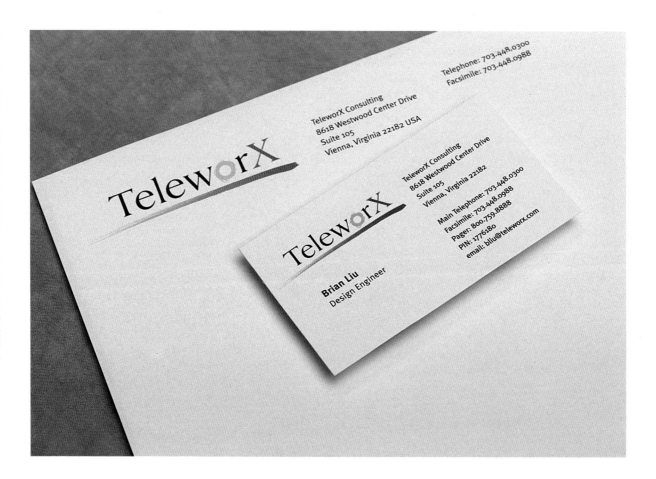

Robert H. Loftur-Thun
Chief Executive Officer

2030 M Street NW, Suite 400, Washington, DC 20036
tel 202 775.0894   **fax** 202 775.1288
e mail ir000336@interramp.com

Logo and Identity

As its primary audience is upscale businesspersons, the overall identity of this cable television channel is conservative. Deep blue and red on stark-white letterhead further add to its buttoned-down look. The mark, however, at once suggestive of the Earth and the letterform "G," gives the identity a contemporary spin. It reflects the dependency of today's business on global communications and modern technology .

(clockwise from top left)

United States Botanic Garden
Public garden

U-17
Soccer tournament

Discovery Communications, Inc.
Program of Discovery Channel

National Wildlife Federation
Membership program

UNITED STATES

BOTANIC GARDEN

FIFA UNDER·17
WORLD CHAMPIONSHIP

U
17.

THE FIFA/JVC CUP
ECUADOR '95

NATIONAL
WILDLIFE
FEDERATION

STUDENT
MEMBERSHIP
PROGRAM

NILE

RIVER
of GODS

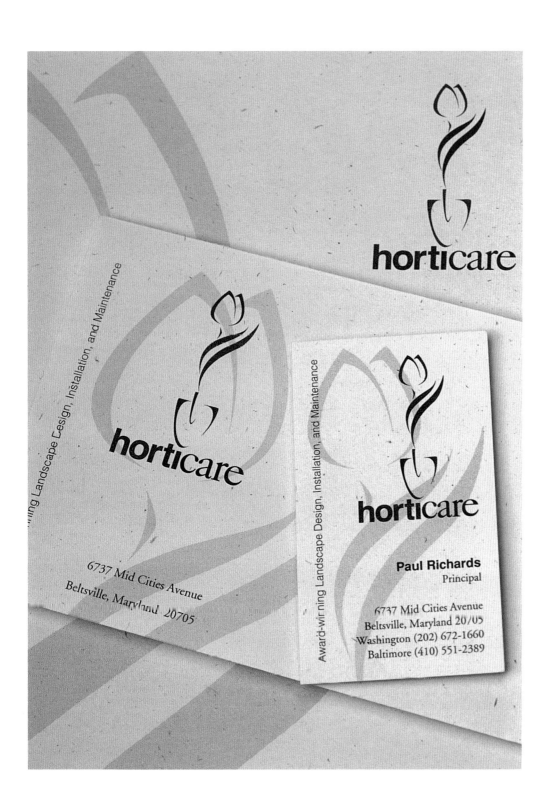

Logo and Identity

A landscape design firm (as opposed to a nursery or a garden shop), HortiCare felt it important to portray itself as such. This logo—both elegant and whimsical—demonstrates that artistry and a strong sense of design are as important for a landscaper's blueprints for outdoor space as they are for an architect's building or an interior designer's room.

**Discovery Online
Identity**

As Discovery
Communications
became increasingly
active on the Internet,
a separate identity
for Discovery Online
was developed.
A magenta border
and full-color icons
connecting people
with technology are
consistent with the
cable channel's
preference for photo-
graphic imagery in
most of its print
communications.

THE WANA ZOO, IN THAILAND, ASKED US TO UPDATE THEIR IDENTITY SYSTEM IN ANTICIPATION OF THEIR GRAND OPENING. WE BUILT ON THEIR BUSINESS-LIKE LOGO, USING THE EXISTING TYPE AS A STARTING POINT BUT ADDING COLOR AND DRAWINGS OF ANIMALS TO BETTER CONVEY A SENSE OF THE CLIENT'S ESSENCE. THE NEW LOOK CAPTURES THE FUN AND EXCITEMENT OF THE ZOO, SUGGESTING THAT IT IS A GREAT PLACE FOR BOTH CHILDREN AND ADULTS—A PLACE WHERE SINGLE YOUNG PEOPLE AND ENTIRE FAMILIES ALIKE CAN FIND ENJOYMENT. AN IMAGE THAT WOULD APPEAL TO ALL AGE GROUPS WAS NEEDED, AS WAS A MULTI-PURPOSE LOOK TRANSLATABLE TO (AND REPRODUCIBLE IN) A WIDE VARIETY OF CONTEXTS AND ENVIRONMENTS, INCLUDING SIGNAGE, INSTITUTIONAL LETTERHEAD, AND GIFT-SHOP MERCHANDISE. OUR SOLUTION INVOLVED USING MANY DIFFERENT ANIMALS WITH THE LOGO, BUT MAKING THEM INTERCHANGEABLE—A UNIQUE AND APPROPRIATE CHOICE, GIVEN THE DIVERSITY OF ANIMALS IN THE ZOO.

Logo and Identity

The new logo which Supon Design Group created for Thailand's Wana Zoo uses typography similar to that of the Zoo's original mark, but with line drawings of animals designed to appeal to both children and adults. The playful, hieroglyphic-style logo varies; in one application, it may be a lion, in another, a rhinoceros, monkey, or snake. Oftentimes, many illustrations are used together to form a delightful pattern.

W A N A   Z O O

W A N A   Z O O   W A N A   Z O O

Entrance Tickets

Since no two visits to the Zoo could be exactly alike, each admission ticket shows a different set of animals, echoing the attraction in all its living variety.

Signage

Directional signage
and banners for
the Zoo can be
understood by both
children and adults,
due to their picto-
graphic style. The
child who can't read
the words "Reptile
House" nonetheless
understands where
to find turtles,
lizards, and snakes.

**Various
Applications**

Among the items
available in the
Zoo's gift shop,
these stationery
items and T-shirts
(shown on opposite
page) are some of
our favorites. They
enable visitors to
take home a little of
the Zoo's exoticism
and magic.

Shopping Bag

This elegant, under-stated shopping bag makes the zoo's logo its main focus by surrounding it with a field of white. The ubiquitous animal pattern with its black background is relegated to the sides for a touch of class.

(clockwise from top left)

The Coca-Cola Company
Portable cold-pack product

Victoria
Health spa

National Trust for Historic Preservation
Program award

United States Department of Agriculture
Federal Agency

Logo and Identity

Paradise Wild is a retail store which sells nature- and animal-related gift items. The store's jungle-inspired identity, shown here on its dramatic stationery, was also applied to shopping bags, signage, and other items.

Logo and Identity

As if saying, "Eureka! I've found the perfect image," a human figure raises his arms in victory in this logo for an organization which provides research assistance for photography. On the envelope, an enlargement of that "perfect image" frames the addressee's name.

Logo and Identity

Stationery was just one application of the Washington Courier logo. The art features several of Washington, D.C.'s well known monuments, but in a non-traditional, illustrative style. The short, quick brush strokes suggest the speed at which the courier service makes its deliveries.

Logo and Identity

Silent Solutions provides computer systems consulting, design, and installation. Its logo transforms from a positive image to a negative one and back again. This, combined with gradations of color as well, suggests the complex subtleties of this line of business.

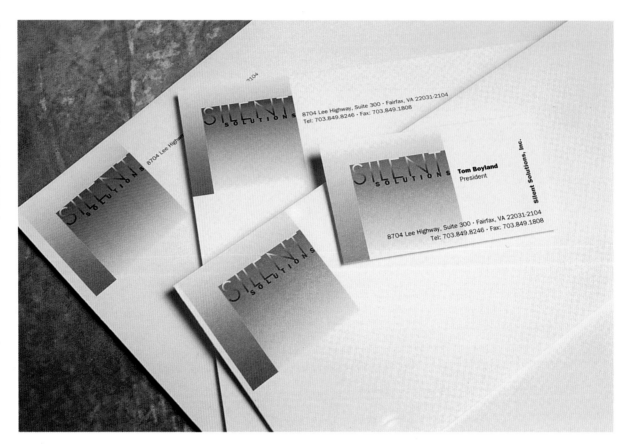

Marketing Materials

A newly opened attraction in the Washington, D.C., area, Newseum is the world's only interactive museum of news. Visitors can relive yesterday's headlines as they learn about the relation between freedom and the press. The covers of each of Newseum's promotional materials portray full-color images layered heavily with illustrative graphics onto full-bleed covers. These convey the depth of issues, information, and activities available at the high-tech museum.